JOE BURROW BIOGRAPHY

How A Small-town Kid Became A Football Hero

Williams A. James

Joe Burrow

TABLE OF CONTENT

INTRODUCTION

Welcome! Are you ready to meet a real-life sports hero who shows that even small towns can have big dreams? So grab a snack and settle down. Joe Burrow was a child who played football with his friends and is now a world-famous player. So get ready for a satisfying read! His story is full of heartbreak, thrills, and touchdowns.

Joe wasn't born in a fancy city where everyone loves football and stadium lights are always on. Not at all! It was a small town in Ohio where Joe grew up. Everyone knows your name, and Joe's goals were the only thing bigger than the sky. He did the same things every other kid did: went to school, hung out with friends, and played football in the yard. But Joe stood out because he had a deep-seated love for football that only grew stronger over time.

When Joe was just a little kid, he wasn't thinking about becoming a sports champion. He was just having fun, playing games, and running around like any other active boy. But then something clicked! Joe discovered football, and suddenly, it wasn't just a game anymore—it was a "passion"! Whether it was throwing the ball, getting it, or running down the field, football quickly became Joe's favorite thing to do.

And guess what? Even though Joe was from a small town, his dreams were anything but small. He pictured playing under the bright stadium lights, hearing the crowd roar, and leading his team to win. The road to getting there wasn't easy, but Joe was ready for the task.

As Joe grew up, so did his skills on the football field. In "high school", he started turning heads. His passes became quicker, his throws harder, and his moves smoother. Coaches and players began to understand that Joe wasn't just a normal player—he was something "special". But here's the thing: Joe didn't get there by chance. He wasn't just naturally amazing at football. Joe worked really, really hard! He trained for hours, never letting up, even when things were tough. That's what made him so great.

One of the coolest parts of Joe's story is how he kept shocking everyone. When he got to "college", he joined the LSU Tigers football team, and that's where everything exploded for him! Imagine this: in his first year at LSU, he led his team to a national title! That means they were the "best" team in all of college sports! Who was in the center of it all? Joe Burrow. He threw passes so perfectly, it was like magic. His comfort on the field grew, and soon everyone knew his name.

Winning the title was huge, but Joe didn't stop there. Oh no, his journey was just getting started. In fact, his story was about to get even more exciting. After college, Joe was ready for the NFL, the place where all the best football players go to fight. And guess what? Joe didn't just join any team—he was picked by the Cincinnati Bengals as their number one draft pick. Imagine that: going from a small town kid to being the number one choice in the NFL draft! It resembled a dream realized.

But let me tell you something amazing about Joe. Even though he's a star player, Joe never lets fame go to his head. He's known for being "humble" and always thinking about others. He's a true team player, and he's always there for his friends, cheering them on and helping them get better. He knows that being a talented football player isn't just about winning games—it's about working together and bringing up the people around you. That's what makes Joe more than just a player; it makes him a leader.

And that's not all! Joe also cares about his "community". He loves helping people and giving back, especially to the people in his hometown who've backed him from the beginning. Whether he's raising money for charities, meeting kids in hospitals, or making inspiring talks, Joe is always thinking of ways to make the world a better place. He proves that heroes are people after the game, not just athletes.

Now, as you turn the pages of this book, you're going to learn even more about Joe Burrow's amazing journey. You'll see how he found football, how he pushed himself to be the best he could be, and how he never let failures stop him from reaching his goals. You'll get to know the "funny" side of Joe, the busy side, and the part of him that loves to laugh and enjoy life with his friends and family.

Joe's story proves you can achieve anything, no matter your background or goals. He's a bright example of what happens when you put your heart and soul into something you love. So, if you've ever thought of doing something great—whether it's on the football field, in the classroom, or anywhere else—Joe's story will inspire you to go for it!

CHAPTER 1: JOE BURROW'S EARLY YEARS AND BACKGROUND

Joe Burrow didn't start out as the outstanding football player we know today. Before all the bright lights and big games, Joe was just a normal kid growing up in a small town, having fun with his family and friends. His story starts in "Athens, Ohio", where Joe was born on "November 10, 1996". It was a place where life was simple but full of love and excitement.

Athens is a town where everybody knows each other. The streets are calm, houses are close, and the air smells like fresh grass, especially in the spring. That's where Joe Burrow grew up. Athens is not the kind of place where you'd expect a future hero to come from, but for Joe, it was the right place to start his journey. Life was easy, but that didn't mean it wasn't full of excitement.

As a child, Joe was always on the move. He loved being outside, running through the garden, and playing with his friends. Whether it was climbing trees, riding bikes, or playing tag, Joe was always up for an adventure. He wasn't the type of kid who wanted to sit inside watching TV all day—nope, Joe loved being busy! His family used to joke that Joe had so much energy, it was like he was driven by a never-ending battery.

Speaking of family, Joe's home was full of love and support. His parents, Jimmy and Robin Burrow, always pushed Joe to try new things and follow his heart. Joe wasn't the only one with a love for sports in the family. His dad, Jimmy, was a football teacher, and Joe looked up to him a lot. Even though he was just a kid, Joe loved watching his dad work with teams, and he learned from him without even realizing it. His dad's love for the game and the way he treated his players stuck with Joe, teaching him about hard work and respect from a very young age.

But football wasn't the only thing on Joe's mind back then. In fact, when he was little, Joe wasn't obsessed with football at all! He loved playing all kinds of games. Sometimes he would toss a ball around with friends, but on other days, he might be riding his bike through the neighborhood or playing basketball at the local court. Joe was the type of kid who loved trying new things. It wasn't just sports either—Joe also liked reading books, playing video games, and even doing school projects. He was a well-rounded kid, curious about the world and always looking for something enjoyable to do.

One of Joe's favorite things to do as a little kid was spend time with his brothers. Joe had two older brothers, "Jamie" and "Dan", who were always there to test him and push him to do better. Whether they were playing games together or just hanging out at home, Joe looked up to his brothers a lot. They helped him be tough, never give up, and most importantly, have fun in everything.

Sometimes, Joe would find himself in fun games with his brothers. They would play basketball or have races in the yard, and even though Joe was younger, he never backed down from a dare. Those little games with his brothers were some of Joe's first experiences with competition, and he loved every second of it. Joe wasn't afraid to lose because he knew that every time he fell, he'd get back up even stronger. He learned to be patient, improve, and always smile.

Growing up in Athens also meant that Joe got to be part of a tight-knit society. People in Athens were always there to help one another, and Joe's family was no different. Joe learned from his parents how to be kind and considerate of others, which he carried throughout his life. Since helping a friend in need and cheering someone on, Joe learned that it's not just what you do—it's how you lift others up.

Even in school, Joe was known for being kind, hardworking, and a loyal friend. His teachers loved him because he was always curious and eager to learn new things. Joe didn't just want to be successful at sports; he wanted to do well in everything he tried. Joe's peers enjoyed being around him because he always had a smile on his face and was ready to include everyone in whatever game or activity he was doing. He was the kind of kid who made sure nobody felt left out, and that made him special.

Joe's early years in Athens were filled with the kind of memories that shaped him into the person he would become. From running around in the backyard with his brothers to learning important lessons from his parents and community, Joe's childhood was all about having fun, trying his best, and always being kind to others.

Even though he hadn't yet found his love for football, the ideals Joe learned growing up in Athens—like hard work, kindness, and never letting up—would stay with him forever. They were the foundation for everything he would go on to accomplish, and they made Joe the outstanding person he is today.

Joe's Family and Home Life

Welcome to the world of Joe Burrow's family, where love, fun, and a little bit of trouble make up every day! Imagine a cozy house in Athens, Ohio, where the Burrow family lives. This isn't just any home; it's a place where fun times and unforgettable moments are always right around the corner.

Joe Burrow was born into a family that was as close-knit as you could imagine. His parents, Jimmy and Robin, were like the best team ever. Jimmy was Joe's dad, and he had a big job as a football coach, but when he was home, he was all about spending time with his family. Robin, Joe's mom, was like a supermom. She juggled taking care of the house, helping with school projects, and cheering Joe on, no matter what. Both of them were always there for Joe, making sure he knew how much they loved him.

The burrow house was always buzzing with activity. The family didn't have to wait for a special event to have fun. They made daily times special, whether it was a weekend breakfast with pancakes stacked high or a cozy movie night with popcorn and blankets. The kitchen was the heart of the house, where Joe's mom would whip up delicious meals, and the family would meet around the table to talk about their day. Imagine the smell of cookies baking in the oven, as well as the sound of laughter ringing through the house. This was a normal day in the burrow home.

Joe had two awesome "brothers", Jamie and Dan, who were not just family but also his best friends. Jamie, the oldest, was always up for a game or journey. He loved playing with Joe and showing him new things, even if it meant getting a little bit dirty. Dan, the third brother, was like a partner in crime. Together, the three of them would come up with all sorts of fun activities, from building forts out of blankets and pillows to organizing backyard sports events. Their house was like a big playground where fantasy ruled the day.

Every day in the burrow home was filled with activities and joy. Joe and his brothers practiced by coming up with new games and tasks. Sometimes, they would pretend to be superheroes, saving the world from imagined enemies. Other times, they'd play "explorers," going on make-believe adventures in their own backyard. The family's big backyard was ideal for all sorts of outdoor fun, and Joe's parents loved watching their kids play and explore.

Joe's family wasn't just about fun and games, though. They were also very close and helpful. Whenever Joe had a big moment, whether it was a school project or a special event, his family was always there to cheer him on. They believed in each other's dreams and worked hard to support one another. Joe's dad, Jimmy, would often share stories from his own youth, teaching Joe about the values of hard work and determination in a way that was both enjoyable and inspiring.

Even though they had busy lives, the Burrow family made sure to spend important time together. They loved having family dinners where they'd share stories from their day and play silly games. Sometimes, they'd take trips to nearby parks or go on family walks, enjoying nature and each other's company. These trips were special times that helped the Burrow family grow even closer.

The Burrow home was also a place where kindness and caring were always in the air. Joe's friends taught him the importance of being kind to others and helping out whenever he could. Whether it was giving a hand to a friend or working for a community event, Joe learned from a young age that being a charitable person was just as important as having fun. This loving nature was something Joe took with him everywhere he went, making him not just a beloved family member but also a wonderful friend to those around him.

One thing that made Joe's home life extra special was how much everyone loved and respected each other. The Burrow family was a team, working together to make their home a joyful and loving place. They praised each other's successes, supported each other during tough times, and always had each other's backs. It was a home filled with hugs, laughs, and lots of love—a wonderful place for Joe to grow up and learn about the world.

His Hobbies and Interests

When Joe Burrow was a kid, he wasn't just about school and sports—he had a bunch of hobbies and interests that made his life extra fun and exciting! Let's take a peek into what made Joe's free time so special and how he filled his days with all sorts of cool activities.

One of Joe's most favorite activities was playing outside. Athens, Ohio, where Joe grew up, had a big, green garden that was nearly a playground for him and his friends. Imagine a place where you can run as fast as you want, climb trees, and make up games—that's what Joe's garden was like. On sunny days, you could find Joe and his friends making the yard into an adventure land. They'd pretend to be explorers looking for hidden wealth or superheroes saving the day from imagined foes. Joe's mind was like a magic wand that turned routine days into epic quests.

Joe also loved "riding his bike" around the neighborhood. With the wind in his hair and the feeling of freedom, biking was one of Joe's favorite ways to spend time. He and his friends would race up and down the streets, seeing who could pedal the fastest. Sometimes they'd have bike tricks events, trying to do wheelies and flips. Every ride was a new adventure, and Joe's bike was his trusted friend.

"Playing basketball was another hobby Joe was really into.] Now, while Joe might not have been the biggest kid on the block, he had a huge love for the game. He'd often grab a basketball and head to the local court, where he'd practice hitting hoops or playing games with his buddies. Joe didn't just enjoy playing basketball; he loved learning new tricks and perfecting his shots. It wasn't just about winning games; it was about having fun and getting better with every bounce of the ball.

When he wasn't outside, Joe enjoyed "reading books". He loved falling into stories and getting lost in different places. From exciting journeys to humorous tales, Joe's books were like magical doors that took him to places far beyond his garden. He'd often curl up with a delightful book and let his mind take flight. Reading was a way for Joe to discover new ideas and stories, and it also helped him learn and grow.

Joe had a knack for building things, too. Whether it was making forts out of blankets and pillows or building elaborate LEGO creations, Joe's creativity knew no limits. He would spend hours planning and making, always coming up with new ideas for his next project. His bedroom was like a small workshop where Joe's mind could run wild. Working with his brain and hands to make something cool and special was Joe's goal.

"Playing video games" was another one of Joe's favorite hobbies. After a day full of outdoor adventures and artistic projects, Joe would sometimes wind down with his favorite video games. He loved getting involved in different game worlds, solving problems, and going on virtual journeys. Video games were a beneficial way for Joe to relax and enjoy some rest while still keeping his mind sharp and active.

Joe was also quite the "music lover". He liked listening to his favorite songs and sometimes even tried his hand at playing musical instruments. Music was an important part of his life, giving a rhythm to his days and making him feel joyful and energetic. Whether he was dancing around the living room or just relaxing with some tunes, music always had a special place in Joe's heart.

Joe's hobbies weren't just about having fun; they were also about learning new things and finding what he loved. His time spent exploring the garden, riding his bike, playing sports, reading, building, games, and listening to music helped shape him into the person he would become. Each of these hobbies gave him important lessons, like how to be artistic, how to work hard, and how to enjoy life to the fullest.

In Joe's world, sports were more than just activities—they were events ready to happen. Each one gave him joy and a sense of achievement. Whether it was a relaxing bike race, an exciting basketball game, or a quiet moment with a delightful book, Joe's hobbies helped him grow and have fun in his own special way. And who knows? All those hobbies might have helped Joe discover some of the traits that would make him a star in his future.

CHAPTER 2: HOW JOE DISCOVERED FOOTBALL

Imagine a kid running around, thinking of journeys, and playing all sorts of games. That's exactly what Joe Burrow was doing until one day he stumbled upon something that would change his life forever—football! It wasn't a big, dramatic moment with fireworks or anything like that. It was just Joe, being his interested self, who found a game that would soon become his favorite.

It all started when Joe was still quite young. He was always busy and loved playing different sports, but football wasn't on his mind just yet. One sunny afternoon, Joe was hanging out in his backyard, playing with his friends, and having a blast. His dad, Jimmy, who was a football teacher, was out there too, working some drills with the neighborhood kids. Joe's eyes were glued to the activity. He watched as the kids ran around, threw the ball, and scored. It looked like so much fun

Joe's dad had always talked about sports, but Joe had never really paid much attention. He knew it was a big deal for his dad, but he was more focused on his own games and adventures. That day, though, something clicked. Joe felt a spark of interest. The way the football soared through the air, and the way the players dashed across the field—it all seemed amazing and exciting. Joe thought, "Hey, that looks like something I'd like to try.

The next day, Joe decided to give football a shot. He asked his dad if he could join in on the practice. Jimmy was thrilled and gave Joe a football, showing him the basics. At first, Joe was a bit wobbly with the ball, trying to figure out how to throw it and catch it. But with his dad's help and a lot of practice, Joe started to get the hang of it. It wasn't long before he was running around, throwing passes, and having a fantastic time.

One of the best things about discovering football was that Joe didn't just enjoy playing it; he also loved watching it. Whenever there was a game on TV, Joe would sit with his family and cheer for his favorite teams. He learned all about the rules, the plays, and the excitement of a close game. Joe enjoyed playing football because he was part of something bigger and shared it with his family.

Joe's love for football grew stronger with every practice. He would spend hours in the garden, practicing his throws and running drills. He'd set up small goals and pretend he was in a big game, running with the ball and scoring fake scores. Joe's excitement was contagious, and his friends and family could see how much fun he was having.

Soon enough, Joe joined a neighborhood football team. At first, he was a little nervous, meeting new partners and learning how to play in a more controlled setting. But his joy and drive quickly helped him fit right in. Joe trained hard, learned new skills, and started to understand the methods of the game. It wasn't just about having fun anymore; it was about working together with his team and improving every day.

One thing that Joe found was that football wasn't just a game; it was a way to make friends and learn important skills. He learned about teamwork, leadership, and the importance of working hard to meet goals. Joe found out that football wasn't just about getting scores; it was about backing his friends and sharing their wins together.

Joe's love for football grew with each game and practice. He loved the feeling of running with the ball, the thrill of making a fantastic play, and the joy of hearing his friends cheer. Football became a huge part of Joe's life, and he couldn't get enough of it. His family and friends saw how much he enjoyed the game and were excited to support him every step of the way.

As Joe continued to play and train, he understood that football was more than just a hobby—it was something he wanted to pursue seriously. His love for the game kept growing, and he knew that he wanted to become the best player he could be. Football wasn't just a hobby; it was a love that drove him to work hard and never give up.

Discovering football was a memorable moment in Joe's life. It was like finding a new adventure that was just waiting for him. From the first time he picked up a football to the endless hours spent training and playing, Joe's journey into the world of football was filled with excitement and joy. Football gave him a new way to have fun, make friends, and chase his dreams. And as Joe continued to play, he knew that this was just the beginning of an exciting and gratifying trip.

Joe's First Big Game

Imagine the butterflies dancing in your stomach before a big event. That's how Joe Burrow felt before his very first big football game. It was a beautiful Saturday morning, and the joy in the air was almost like a magic spell. Joe was excited to play his first real game after planning it for a long time.

The game was played on the local field, which looked like a big green playground. The stands were packed with parents, friends, and neighbors, all cheering and clapping. Joe's heart raced as he walked onto the field, holding his football helmet in one hand and his water bottle in the other. The smell of fresh grass and the sound of excited talk filled the air, making Joe's excitement even bigger.

As Joe put on his helmet and fixed his pads, he felt like he was going into a world full of excitement. His outfit was shiny and new, and he couldn't wait to show off his skills. He had practiced so hard for this moment, and now it was time to put all of his practice into action.

The whistle blew, and the game began. Joe's team grouped up, and their coach gave them a pep talk, telling them to play their best and have fun. Joe listened carefully, feeling the excitement and support from his friends. Everyone was pumped up and ready to

Joe started the game on the benches, watching as his friends dashed around, catching passes, and making outstanding plays. He was filled with a mix of nervousness and joy. This was the moment he'd been waiting for!He couldn't wait to get onto the field and show everyone what he could do.

When Joe's turn finally came, he ran onto the field with a big grin on his face. His boss called his name, and Joe felt like a superhero ready to save the day. He lined up with his friends and got into position. They snapped the ball, and play started. Joe raced down the field, feeling the rush of the game and the crowd's cheers. It was like being in the middle of an action-packed movie.

Joe's first big play was a pass. The quarterback threw the ball toward him, and for a moment, time seemed to slow down. Joe reached out, stretching his hands towards the ball. He caught it with a pleasant thud and started running, his heart racing with excitement. The crowd cheered, and Joe's friends yelled words of support. It was an amazing feeling to be part of such an exciting game.

As the game went on, Joe continued to give it his all. He ran with the ball, made some awesome stops, and even scored a touchdown. The cheers from the stands got louder, and Joe couldn't believe how much fun he was having. Every play was an adventure, and Joe felt like he was living his dream.

One of the best parts of Joe's first big game was how much he liked playing with his friends. They were all out there, working together, having fun, and cheering each other on. When Joe got his first touchdown, his friends ran over to celebrate with him. They high-fived and hugged, and Joe felt like he was part of a fantastic team. The joy of playing with friends made the game even more special.

Even though Joe's team didn't win the game, Joe felt like a winner. He had given it his best shot and had a blast doing it. The game was full of exciting moments, and Joe had learned so much. His football experience taught him that it was about having fun, playing hard, and being a team. Joe's first big game was a wonderful adventure, full of laughter, cheers, and amazing memories.

When the final whistle blew, Joe's team gathered around their boss for a post-game chat. They talked about the game, what went well, and what they could do better. Joe felt proud of himself and his friends. They had played with heart and had a great time; that was what mattered.

Big Joe Learning to Love the Sport

Imagine finding something that makes you feel like you're on top of the world—a special activity that makes you smile every time you think about it. That's exactly how Joe Burrow felt as he grew more and more in love with football. It wasn't just a game to him; it was an exciting journey that he looked forward to every day.

Joe's journey of learning to love football began with the simple joy of playing. Initial enjoyment came from running, catching, and scoring touchdowns. But as Joe trained more and played in different games, he started to understand something even more exciting: football was not just about having fun—it was also about pushing himself and getting better every day.

Joe Burrow

Joe's favorite thing about football was the feeling of growth. Every time he practiced, he got a little bit better. Whether it was perfecting a tricky throw, running faster, or learning new plays, Joe felt a sense of success with every step forward. It was like solving a puzzle—each new skill he learned made him more excited about the game.

Joe loved the thrill of learning new moves. He spent countless hours training his footwork, working on his throwing skill, and learning different moves. He'd often set up small drills in his garden, pretending he was in a big game. With every pass and every run, Joe felt more linked to the sport. It was like he was finding a new ability with each practice session.

Another reason Joe grew to love football was "teamwork. Football wasn't just about one person; it was about working together as a team. Joe found joy in teaming up with his friends and playing in a group. They would train together, share tips, and cheer each other on. The feeling of being part of a team, encouraging one another, and enjoying victories together made football even more important to Jo.

Joe's coaches and teammates played a big role in his growing love for the sport. His teachers were like guides who helped him learn the game and improve his skills. They supported him, gave him tips, and helped him understand football's methods. Joe respected their dedication and was moved by their love for the game. In the game, his teammates were his friends and partners. They shared his excitement, worked hard together, and made playing football even more fun.

"Watching football games" on TV also helped Joe fall in love with the sport. He loved seeing the big plays, the cheering crowds, and the excitement of the game. He'd often watch games with his family and try to copy the moves of his best players. It was like getting a front-row seat to the action and learning new skills from the best. As he watched, he wanted to join the thrilling act.

Joe also found that "football was a way to challenge himself". He loved setting goals and pushing himself to reach them. Whether it was improving his speed, learning a new play, or handling a tricky pass, Joe loved the challenge. Each goal he achieved made him feel pleased and excited to keep going. Football became a way for him to test his abilities and see how far he could go.

Joe's favorite part of football was the feeling of getting a touchdown. There was nothing like the rush of running into the end zone and hearing the cheers from the crowd. It made all the hard work and practice feel worth it. Every touchdown was a party, and Joe loved the thrill of crossing the finish line and making his team happy.

As Joe continued to play, he understood that football wasn't just a sport; it was a "source of happiness" and energy. It gave him something to look forward to, a way to express himself, and a chance to be part of something bigger than himself. It was more than a game—he loved football.

Learning to love football was like finding a new world full of excitement, difficulties, and fun. Joe's trip was filled with times of excitement, hard work, and joy. He found joy in every practice, excitement in every game, and a deep love for the sport that would stay with him forever. Football became a big part of Joe's life, and he couldn't wait to see where his love for the game would take him next.

CHAPTER 3: JOE BURROW'S HIGH SCHOOL DREAMS

High school is a time of big dreams, new obstacles, and finding out who you really are. For Joe Burrow, it was a time filled with hope, drive, and the thrill of chasing his sports dreams. Joe wasn't just playing football for fun anymore; he was thinking big and working hard to make those dreams come true.

When Joe started high school, he was ready for a new journey. His high school had a fantastic football team, and Joe was excited to join and show everyone what he could do. He was eager to make a name for himself and help his team win games. High school football was like moving into a new world where every game was a chance to shine.

Joe's high school football team was known for its energy and excitement. The field was always buzzing with energy, and the seats were full with cheering fans. Joe loved the feeling of being part of such a lively team. It was like being in a big, lively family where everyone supported each other and worked together to reach their goals.

During practice, Joe was all about working hard and giving his best. He spent hours running sprints, improving his throws, and learning new plays. His practice sessions were like little journeys where he explored new skills and found ways to improve. Joe knew that the more work he put in, the better he'd become. Each practice was a chance to learn and grow, and Joe loved every minute of it.

One of the most exciting parts of high school football was the Friday night games. The mood at these games was exciting! The field lights would shine bright, the crowd would roar with excitement, and Joe would feel a rush of energy as he stepped onto the field. These games were the highlight of the week, and Joe looked forward to them with a big smile on his face. The thrill of playing in front of so many people and the joy of scoring touchdowns made every game a special adventure.

Joe's hopes for high school football went beyond just playing well. He wanted to be a leader on the field. He worked hard to be a beneficial partner, helping his friends improve and cheering them on. Joe knew that being a stellar player wasn't just about making amazing plays; it was also about inspiring others and building a positive team spirit. He took pride in supporting his peers and enjoying their accomplishments.

As the season continued, Joe's skills and confidence grew. He became known for his amazing plays and his never-give-up approach. He loved the task of each game and the excitement of every play. Joe's hard work had paid off, and he was starting to catch the attention of agents and trainers. It felt wonderful to see his dreams taking shape, and Joe was thrilled to be on the path to achieving them.

Outside of practice and games, Joe spent time "watching football games" and studying his favorite players. He loved learning new methods and skills from watching the pros. It was like getting extra tips and tricks to help him improve. Joe would often practice moves he saw on TV, imagining himself making those amazing plays on the field. This extra work helped him improve his skills and stay inspired.

Joe's high school dreams also included combining his sports goals with his schoolwork. He knew that being a good student was also important. Joe worked hard to keep up with his studies while chasing his sports dreams. Because he valued school and sports equally, he worked hard in both. His attention to his studies and his sport demonstrated that he could handle the challenges of high school with drive and focus.

Joe's family and friends helped him a lot during his high school journey. They were always there to cheer him on, whether he was on the field or preparing for a big game. Their support and belief in him gave Joe the strength to keep pushing towards his dreams. He knew that having people who cared about him made all the difference.

Joe's high school years were a time of energy, hard work, and thinking big. He loved the thrill of playing football, the task of improving his skills, and the joy of being part of a team. Each game, each practice, and each moment of support from his family and friends made his high school journey special and unforgettable.

Playing for His High School Team

Being on his high school football team was like going into a world of excitement and adventure for Joe Burrow. From the time he joined the team, every day was a new chance to learn, play, and grow. Let's take a closer look at what made Joe's high school sports experience so special.

Joe's high school football team was full of energy and spirit. The team wore bright outfits that sparkled under the stadium lights, and Joe felt like a star every time he put on his shirt. The outfit's colors made him feel strong and ready to tackle any task. His mask and pads were like armor, covering him and making him feel like a real fighter on the field.

Every practice was a mix of hard work and fun. Joe and his friends trained on a big, green field that looked like their own private playground. The field had lines, goal posts, and a shiny sign that added to the excitement. Practice sessions were like treasure hunts, where Joe looked for ways to improve his skills and become a better player. The drills were filled with laughter and cheers as the team worked together to learn new moves and skills.

Joe's teachers were like guides on this journey. They helped him understand the game better and showed him new ways to play. Whether it was perfecting a tricky pass or learning a new plan,

Joe listened carefully to their tips and tried his best to apply them. The coaches' support and tips made Joe feel strong and excited to improve with every practice.

Team huddles were one of the best aspects of being on the team. Before every play, the players would meet in a close circle, hands in the middle, and listen to the coach's directions. The group was powered by electricity. Joe loved the feeling of togetherness and teamwork. The cheers, high-fives, and shouts of excitement made him feel like he was part of something truly special. The team huddles were a beautiful moment before the big play, where everyone was focused and ready to give their all.

"Game days" were like the big end to a fun journey. Fridays were especially exciting because they meant a big game was coming up. The stadium was packed with people cheering loudly, and the smell of popcorn and hot dogs filled the air. The bright lights made everything look lively and exciting. Joe and his friends would run onto the field, and the roar of the crowd made his heart race. The feeling of being part of a big event was amazing, and Joe loved every bit of it.

Each game was like a new quest. Joe and his friends worked hard to put their practice into action. The games were full of obstacles, and Joe liked finding out how to beat the opponents. Every play was a chance to show off the skills they had been training. Whether it was a bold pass, a strong hit, or a quick run, Joe felt like he was living out his football goals. The thrill of making a wonderful play and hearing the cheers from the crowd was amazing.

One of Joe's best times was when he scored a touchdown. The play began with a snap of the ball, and Joe got into position. He ran with all his might, made a beautiful catch, and dashed towards the end zone. As he crossed the line, the crowd burst in cheers. Scoring a touchdown felt like winning a mini-celebration. Joe loved the feeling of joy and success that came with every score.

But playing football wasn't just about the games. It was also about the ties and memories made along the way. Joe and his friends shared many fun times together. They socialized, joked, and supported each other off the field. The bond they shared made playing and training even more enjoyable. Whether it was enjoying a win or planning the next game, Joe valued the time spent with his friends.

After the games, the team would often meet to talk about the day's events. They'd chat about what went well, what could be better, and share their favorite moments from the game. These post-game talks were filled with laughs and friendship. Joe loved hearing his teammates' stories and sharing his own. It was a time to think about their travels and enjoy the thrill of the game.

Joe's high school football experience was full of energy, difficulties, and fun. He loved the feeling of being part of a team, working hard to improve, and enjoying the game's joys. Each practice and game was a chance to learn and grow, and Joe welcomed every moment with excitement. Playing for his high school team was an amazing adventure, and Joe was grateful for the memories and experiences it brought.

Joe's Hard Work Pays Off

In the world of sports, hard work and determination are like hidden keys to success. For Joe Burrow, these elements mixed together to make a recipe for success. Let's look into how Joe's constant effort and drive during high school led to some amazing successes!

Joe was always the first to arrive and last to leave practice. He treated each practice session like a treasure hunt, looking for ways to improve his game. Every drill was a chance to become better, and Joe was on a mission. He practiced throwing, running, and improving his skills. It wasn't just about hard work; it was about working smart and giving his best every single time.

One of Joe's greatest strengths was facing problems head-on. If he made a mistake or didn't do well in a drill, he didn't get disheartened. Instead, he saw it as a chance to learn and get even better. Joe's attitude was like a superpower—he changed every mistake into a stepping stone towards success. He'd practice those tricky plays over and over until he got them just right. It was like solving a big problem, and Joe was determined to finish it.

Joe's hard work wasn't just about what happened on the field. He spent time watching football games, studying his favorite players, and learning new tactics. This extra schoolwork helped him understand the game better and gave him new ideas to try out during practice. It was like getting extra tips from a coach on TV, and Joe loved adding these new tricks to his toolbox.

As the season continued, Joe's hard work started to show. He began making amazing plays that left fans and teachers cheering. His passes were accurate, his runs were fast, and his hits were strong. Joe's name was becoming well-known, and he started getting honored for his skill and work. It was like his hard work was paying off with golden stars and praise.

Joe led his team to a big win in one game that stood out. It was a difficult game with a tough opponent, but Joe was ready. He put everything he had learned into action. The game was a rollercoaster of excitement, and Joe was at the center of it all. He made an amazing throw that ended in a fantastic touchdown. The crowd went wild, and his friends lifted him up in celebration. It was a moment of pure joy, and it showed how Joe's hard work had led to something truly special.

Joe's commitment didn't go ignored. His teachers praised him for his work and progress. They saw how much he had grown as a player, and how his hard work had made a difference. Joe's friends also praised his dedication. They saw how hard he worked and were moved to push themselves even more. Joe had become a role model, showing everyone that hard work could lead to big things.

Outside of sports, Joe also worked hard in school. He knew that being a good student was also important. Balancing his schoolwork and football training was like balancing two important balls, and Joe managed to keep them both in the air. His teachers noticed his effort and commitment, and they admired how he managed to excel in both areas. Joe's ability to balance his academic and sports responsibilities was another example of his hard work paying off.

The hard work Joe put into football also brought him closer to his dreams. College scouts started noticing his excellent efforts. They saw Joe's promise and were excited about the thought of him playing at the next level. Joe's hard work had opened doors to new possibilities, and he was one step closer to reaching his final goal.

Joe's journey was a wonderful example of how hard work can turn dreams into reality. His commitment, perseverance, and love for sports helped him achieve success and inspire others. Every practice, every game, and every bit of work was a building block towards something amazing. Joe's hard work didn't just lead to wins on the field; it also taught him important lessons about determination and the benefits of never giving up.

CHAPTER 4: JOE BURROW THE COLLEGE FOOTBALL STAR

When Joe Burrow stepped onto his college campus, he knew something special was about to happen. College football was a whole new adventure, and Joe was ready to face it head-on. The crowd was bigger, the games were faster, and the rivalry was tougher, but Joe wasn't scared. He was excited! This was his chance to shine, to show everyone what he was made of, and to live out his sports dreams on the biggest stage yet.

Joe decided to play for "Louisiana State University (LSU), a school known for its loud fans and powerful football team. The mood at LSU was exciting. The moment Joe walked into the stadium, the excitement hit him like a wave. Thousands of fans, all decked out in purple and gold, filled the seats, screaming so loudly it felt like the ground was shaking. It was the right place for someone with big goals, like Joe.

But it wasn't straightforward at first. College football was like a whole new world compared to high school. The players were faster, bigger, and more experienced. Joe had to work even harder to prove himself. But remember, hard work was Joe's secret tool, and he was never one to back down from a task. Every day at practice, Joe pushed himself to be better. He studied the game, practiced harder, and listened carefully to his teachers, taking up all the tips like a sponge.

At first, Joe didn't get to play as much as he wanted. It was tough sitting on the benches, watching his friends take the field. But Joe knew that beneficial things take time. He didn't let sadness stop him. Instead, he kept working. He kept training. And most importantly, he kept believing in himself. Joe knew that one day his moment would come—and when it did, he would be ready.

And oh, did that moment come! When Joe finally got his chance to step onto the field as the starting quarterback, it was like watching a superhero in action. He controlled the game with ease and accuracy, throwing passes that seemed to glide through the air like rockets. His friends trusted him, and the crowd went wild every time he made a big play. It was clear to everyone: Joe Burrow was a star in the making.

One of Joe's most memorable games came when LSU faced a tough opponent. The heat was on, and the stakes were high. But Joe thrived under pressure. The game was intense—back and forth, with both teams giving it their all. But Joe stayed calm and focused. He led his team down the field with smart plays and quick choices. And when the moment came, Joe fired a beautiful pass into the end zone for a game-winning score! The crowd exploded, and Joe's friends ran to celebrate with him. It was a moment of pure joy and victory.

As the season went on, Joe kept impressing everyone with his skills and guidance. He wasn't just good—he was *great*. His ability to read defenses, make quick choices, and throw perfect passes made him one of the best players in college football. His name started showing up in the news, and people everywhere were talking about this young quarterback from LSU who was taking the sports world by storm.

But Joe's journey wasn't just about the big wins. It was about the things he learned along the way. He learned the value of teamwork, how every player on the field had a role to play, and that winning wasn't just about one person—it was about the whole team working together. Joe became a leader, someone his friends could trust both on and off the field. He pulled them up when things were tough and enjoyed their team victories.

Joe also learned the importance of persistence. There were moments when things did not go as expected. Maybe a game didn't turn out the way he wanted, or he made a mistake on the field. But Joe never let those times bring him down. Instead, he utilized them as motivation to strive harder. He knew that success wasn't just about talent—it was about heart, drive, and the willingness to keep going, no matter what.

By the end of his college career, Joe Burrow had become a true football star. He led LSU to an amazing season, breaking records and winning the hearts of fans everywhere. His incredible performances won him the famous "Heisman Trophy", an award given to the best player in college football. Standing on the stage, holding that shiny prize, Joe couldn't help but smile. It was the perfect reminder of how far he had come—from the kid who loved football in his small town to one of the best college players ever.

Joe's time at LSU was an exciting adventure full of challenges, wins, and unforgettable moments. He showed that with hard work, commitment, and a love for the game, anything was possible. His college football journey was just the beginning of something even bigger, and Joe knew that there were still many more exciting pages to come in his football story.

For Joe, college wasn't just about becoming a star. It was about learning, growing, and becoming the best version of himself—both on the field and off. And as his college sports days came to a close, one thing was clear: Joe Burrow was meant for greatness, and the best was yet to come!

How Joe Burrow Joined the LSU Tigers

Joe Burrow had always thought big. And when it came time to choose a college, he made one of the biggest decisions of his life—he picked the "LSU Tigers". Now, if you've ever heard of the LSU Tigers, you know they're not your average football team. These were winners. Legends. And playing for them meant walking onto a field where some of the best players had once stood. Joe wanted to be part of that tradition, even if it meant leaving his small Ohio town and going down south to Louisiana.

So, how did a small-town kid like Joe end up picking LSU, a school so far from home? Well, Joe wasn't afraid of problems. He had played football his whole life, and he knew he was ready for something big. But it wasn't just about playing football—it was about being part of something special. LSU had a reputation, not just for winning but for pushing players to be their very best. Joe's goal was to be the best. So, when LSU knocked, he listened.

When Joe first arrived at LSU, he was in awe. The school was huge, and everyone seemed to live and breathe sports. However, the biggest surprise? "Tiger Stadium", also known as "Death Valley." It was a giant stadium, and when it was full, it could hold more than 100,000 people! Joe had never seen anything like it. Standing in the middle of the field, he thought about what it would feel like to play in front of a crowd that big. His heart raced with excitement. This was the place where sports goals came true, and Joe knew he was ready to make his mark.

But being part of the LSU Tigers wasn't going to be easy. The team was stacked with skilled players, and Joe had to show himself if he wanted to earn a spot. His first practices were tough. The other players were fast, strong, and smart. They knew the game like the back of their hands, and Joe quickly realized he had a lot to learn. But instead of feeling dejected, Joe was fired up. He wasn't afraid of hard work, and he knew that if he pushed himself, he could keep up with the best of the best.

Joe's first few weeks at LSU were filled with early morning workouts, late-night study sessions, and endless hours of watching game videos. It was tiring, but Joe loved it. He loved the work. He enjoyed the feeling of pushing himself to his maximum. And most of all, he loved being part of a team that felt like family. The LSU Tigers weren't just teammates—they were brothers. They pushed each other, supported each other, and enjoyed every small success together.

One of the biggest problems Joe faced was learning LSU's complicated plan. This wasn't just any playbook—it was packed with advanced plays and plans that would make any football player's head spin. But Joe didn't back down. Every night after practice, he would sit down with his script, determined to remember every play and understand every plan. It wasn't easy, but with each passing day, things started to click. Joe was getting smarter, faster, and more confident.

Then came "game day". If you've never been to a college football game at Tiger Stadium, you're missing out! The mood was exciting. The stands were filled with fans dressed in purple and gold, waving flags, and screaming at the top of their voices. The LSU band played the fight song, and the whole stadium seemed to pulse with excitement. Joe could feel the energy in the air as he and his friends ran out onto the field. The noise was so loud, it felt like the ground was shaking beneath them.

Joe knew this was what he had worked for. This was the moment he had thought about his whole life—playing for a top college team, in front of thousands of screaming fans, wearing the LSU shirt. But it wasn't just about the crowd or the cheers. For Joe, it was about being part of something bigger. He wasn't just playing for himself—he was playing for his friends, his teachers, and every fan who believed in him.

But Joe quickly learned that being on a team like LSU wasn't just about fame. It was about hard work, dedication, and never letting up. There were days when practices were tough, and games didn't always go as planned. But Joe never lost sight of his goal. He stayed focused, pushed through the tough times, and always gave his best effort. His teachers noticed his drive, and his friends started to trust him. Slowly but surely, Joe was winning his place on the team.

For Joe, one of the best parts of being an LSU Tiger was the friendship. The players spent so much time together, both on and off the field. They ate meals together, hung out in the locker room, and even helped each other with chores. They weren't simply teammates; they were pals. Joe loved the bond he had with his fellow Tigers. They were always there for each other, whether it was enjoying a big win or picking each other up after a tough loss.

As the season went on, Joe kept improving. He learned from every drill, every game, and every task he faced. And with each passing week, he felt more and more like a true LSU Tiger. He had proven that he belonged, and he was ready to give everything he had to help his team win.

How Joe Winned the Championship!

It was the biggest game of Joe Burrow's life—the College Football National Championship! The air was buzzing with energy, the stadium lights were burning, and thousands of fans were cheering their hearts out. The air was electric, and Joe knew this was his chance. After all the hard work, practice, and commitment, it had all come down to this one game.

Joe stood tall on the field, wearing his purple and gold LSU outfit, cap strapped tight. His heart was beating fast, but he wasn't worried. Joe was ready. He'd dreamed of this day ever since he was a kid, tossing a football in his garden. And now he was about to lead his team, the LSU Tigers, to the most important win of his life.

The other team, the Clemson Tigers, was tough. They were fast, strong, and ready to fight for the win, too. But Joe wasn't afraid. He'd faced problems before, and he knew how to stay calm under pressure. He looked at his friends, giving them a confident nod. They believed in him, and he believed in them. Together, they were going to give it everything they had.

As the official blew the whistle to start the game, Joe took a deep breath and stepped onto the field. The crowd was screaming, but all Joe could hear was the sound of the football being snapped into his hands. It was time to get to work!

The first quarter was a fight. Clemson scored early, and the pressure was on. But Joe didn't worry. He quietly led his team down the field, making one perfect pass after another. The football flew through the air like a rocket, and Joe's players caught it with ease. Every time Joe launched the ball, it felt like magic. On the edge of their seats, LSU Tiger fans watched their comeback.

By halfway, the score was close. Joe and his friends met in the change room, hot but determined. "We've got this," Joe told them. "We've worked too diligently to give up now. Let's go out there and play the best game of our lives!" His words fired up the whole team, and they stormed back onto the field with new energy.

In the second half, Joe was unbeatable. He threw touchdown after touchdown, moving the ball down the field like a true winner. The Clemson defense couldn't keep up. Every time they thought they had Joe caught, he would make a quick pass or run out of the hole, leaving them in the dust.

The crowd was going wild! Fans were waving LSU flags, jumping up and down, and screaming at the top of their lungs. Joe could feel their energy driving him, pushing him to play even harder. He was in the zone, and nothing could stop him now.

Then came the play that would seal the game. It was the fourth quarter, and LSU had the ball on Clemson's 20-yard line. The title was within reach, but they needed one more big play. Joe dropped back to pass, searching the field for an open target. The defense was closing in fast, and the pressure was growing.

But Joe didn't move. With ice in his blood, he shot the ball high into the air. It flew across the field, spinning exactly as it headed toward his wide target in the end zone. The whole crowd held its breath.

Then, "boom"! The ball fell exactly in his teammate's hands for a score! The crowd erupted in cheers, fireworks burst in the sky, and confetti rained down from the stands. The LSU Tigers had done it—they had won the National Championship!

Joe couldn't believe it. He had led his team to win on the biggest stage in college sports. His friends ran onto the field and hugged him, patted him on the back, and pulled him up in joy. Joe held his hat in the air, grinning from ear to ear. It was a moment he would never forget.

The party was huge. Fans were screaming, the LSU fight song was playing, and everywhere Joe looked, people were jumping up and down in joy. His parents were in the stands, beaming with joy. They had watched Joe work so hard for this moment, and now it was finally here. He had made them proud.

As Joe stood on the stage, holding the title prize high above his head, he couldn't help but feel a rush of joy and relief. All the sweat, all the hard work, all the hours spent practicing—it had all paid off. He was a winner, and no one could ever take that away from him.

The powder continued to fall, covering the field in purple and gold. Joe's teammates circled him, praising their amazing success. They had done it together as a team, and that made the win even sweeter. Joe knew he couldn't have done it without them, and he was grateful for every single one of his friends who had fought alongside him.

Even amid the excitement, Joe knew this was just the beginning. Yes, he had won the college football title, but there were still bigger goals to chase. The NFL was calling, and Joe was ready to answer.

As the lights of the stadium shone down on him, Joe smiled. He had come a long way from playing football in his garden. Now, he was a national winner. And while he didn't know exactly what the future held, one thing was for sure: Joe Burrow was going to keep chasing his dreams, and nothing could stop him.

CHAPTER 5: THE NFL JOURNEY OF JOE BURROW

After his big win in the college football title, Joe Burrow knew that his journey wasn't over—it was just starting! The next stop? The NFL, where only the best of the best get to play. Joe had thought about this moment since he was a little kid, throwing footballs in his garden, thinking he was in the Super Bowl. And now that dream was finally coming true!

The NFL Draft was just around the corner, and Joe was excited—and maybe a little worried, too. This was a huge step. Teams from all over the country were going to pick the best college players to join their teams, and Joe knew he had worked hard to show that he belonged at the top. He had made countless perfect passes, led his team to wins, and never gave up, even when things got tough. Now, it was time to see if all that hard work would pay off.

On draft day, Joe sat with his family, watching the big event occur on TV. His heart was beating as one by one, players were picked. Then, the moment finally came—the news that would change his life forever. The Cincinnati Bengals had the "first pick", and guess what? They picked Joe Burrow! The room exploded in cheers, and Joe was grinning from ear to ear. He was headed to the NFL!

Joining the Bengals was like moving into a whole new world. The NFL was different from college. The players were faster and bigger, and the stakes were even higher. But Joe wasn't scared—he was ready to give it his all. From the time he stepped onto the field for his first practice, he knew this was where he belonged. The Bengals accepted him with open arms, and the fans were super excited to see what this new young quarterback could do.

The first game of the season was a big deal. For his NFL debut, Joe felt butterflies in his stomach. The stadium lights were bright, and the roar of the crowd filled the air. It was the kind of moment that every football player dreams about. Joe took a deep breath, put on his helmet, and stepped onto the field, ready to lead his team.

The other team's defense was tough, but Joe was tougher. He stood tall in the pocket, scanning the field for an open target. When he saw his chance, he fired the ball with perfect precision, and the crowd went wild as his partner made the catch! Joe had just thrown his first NFL touchdown, and the fans couldn't get enough of him.

But the NFL road wasn't always easy. There were days when the games didn't go the way Joe had hoped. Some teams were really good at stopping his passes, and there were times when he was knocked down hard. But every time Joe got knocked down, he got right back up. That's the kind of guy Joe was—determined, focused, and never willing to give up, no matter how difficult things got.

The Bengals had a tough season, but Joe kept growing. Every game was a chance to learn, to get better, and to show the world what he was made of. He worked hard at every practice, learning plays, watching films, and improving his throws. He wasn't just playing to win—he was playing to become the best quarterback he could be.

And the Bengals fans noticed. They loved Joe's never-give-up attitude and his cool, calm way of handling pressure. Even when things looked tough, Joe kept his head high and his eyes on the goal. His friends trusted him, and together they began to build something special.

Joe's NFL journey wasn't just about winning games—it was about growing as a player and a leader. In the locker room were veteran NFL players, and Joe wanted to learn from them. He listened carefully to their advice, soaked up their knowledge, and used every chance to improve his game.

One of the best parts of Joe's NFL journey was the amazing love from his friends. Bengals fans were some of the most enthusiastic in the league, and they loved Joe for his toughness, his skill, and his heart. Every time he stepped onto the field, the people cheered him on, waving their orange and black flags and yelling his name. Joe felt like he was playing for more than just himself—he was playing for the entire city of Cincinnati.

As the season went on, Joe kept racking up scores, making jaw-dropping throws, and leading his team to some big wins. But for Joe, it wasn't just about individual success. It was about making his team better and helping the Bengals become a force to be reckoned with in the NFL.

Of course, Joe's journey in the NFL was just starting. He knew there would be more challenges ahead—tougher opponents, bigger games, and times where he would need to dig deep and give it everything he had. But that's exactly what Joe was ready for. He had the heart of a winner, and nothing was going to stop him from chasing his NFL dreams.

The NFL trip wasn't just about football—it was about showing that no matter where you come from, no matter how big the obstacles, with hard work and drive, anything is possible. And Joe Burrow was ready to show the world that he had what it took to become one of the best players in the game.

Joe Burrow Draft Day Excitement

The day had finally arrived—the day every college football star dreams about! It was "Draft Day", and Joe Burrow could hardly control his joy. He felt like a kid on Christmas morning, bursting with joy and expectation. This moment could change his life forever, and he was ready!

As Joe sat in his living room, surrounded by his family, the mood was exciting. The TV was set up, and all eyes were glued to the screen, where fans and reporters were talking about the future picks. The clock was ticking down, and the suspense was almost too much to handle. Joe's heart raced as he thought about the teams that might choose him. Which team would he join? Would he be the first pick? He could hardly wait!

To help calm his worries, Joe's family shared humorous stories about his childhood. They talked about all the times he'd throw a football in the garden, thinking he was leading a team to victory. His folks laughed about how he used to practice his score dance in front of the mirror. "You were always convinced you were going to be a celebrity!" his mom said with a smile. Hearing their laughter made Joe feel warm inside and reminded him of how far he had come.

As the draft started, Joe watched with wide eyes. The camera zoomed in on players in fancy clothes, nervously waiting for their names to be called. Joe felt a mix of joy and nerves. What if he didn't get picked? But he quickly shook off that thought. He had worked hard, practiced every day, and given it his all. He believed in himself!

The first few picks came and went. Each time a name was called, Joe cheered for his fellow players, feeling thrilled for them even as his own heart raced. Then, as the Cincinnati Bengals' turn came, the energy in the room soared. Joe could feel the excitement rising. Would they choose him?

Finally, the moment everyone had been waiting for came. The Bengals were on the clock, and the announcer's voice filled the air: "With the first pick in the 2020 NFL Draft, the Cincinnati Bengals select Joe Burrow, quarterback from LSU!"

Joe's heart soared! He jumped off the couch and did a little joyful dance. His family burst in cheers, hugging him tightly. "You did it! You're going to the NFL!" They shouted, and the joy in the room was incredible. Joe couldn't believe it—his dream was coming true!

As he sat back down, still buzzing with energy, Joe thought about what this meant. He was going to join a professional football team, and he'd get to play the game he loved at the top level. It felt strange! He picked up his phone to call his friends, who had backed him all along. "You won't believe it! I'm finally a Bengal!" He laughed out loud, and the cheers from the other end brought a big smile to his face.

After the news, the parties continued. Joe and his family took shots, grinning from ear to ear. They wore Bengals shirts and held up signs, enjoying the moment. They would never forget that day.

But there was more enjoyment to come! The NFL Draft wasn't just about being picked; it was about the future. Joe pondered training with his new friends, learning from the coaches, and playing in front of thousands. The idea of stepping onto the field in a real NFL game sent chills down his spine. He felt ready for the task!

As the draft continued, Joe watched other players get picked, sharing their excitement as they joined their new teams. Some were jumping up and down, some were crying joyful tears, and others were hugging their families tightly. The rush of emotions made Joe grateful to be there.

When the night was over, Joe sat down to think. This was just the beginning of his NFL journey. He thought about all the hard work he had put in to get here—the tryouts, the long hours, the times of doubt. And now, all of that work had led him to this amazing chance.

As the lights faded and the energy of the day calmed, Joe knew that he had to get to work. The

NFL was a whole new world, and he was ready to dive in headfirst. He thought about his goals, his dreams, and how he wanted to show everyone that he was meant to be there.

That night, Joe went to bed with a smile on his face. He had a big journey ahead, filled with obstacles and successes, but he was ready. Joe Burrow had big dreams, ready to dominate the NFL with his family by his side. Draft Day was just the beginning, and he couldn't wait to see what thrills awaited him on the field!

How He Became a Cincinnati Bengal

Joe Burrow was finally a Cincinnati Bengal! Can you imagine the thrill? It was like stepping into a superhero outfit for the first time, ready to take the world. Except for Joe, his heroic suit was orange and black, with a fierce Bengal tiger roaring on the cap. The moment he put on that shirt, everything felt real. Joe wasn't just thinking about the NFL anymore—he was living it!

From the moment he was chosen, Joe knew things were about to get serious. Joining an NFL team wasn't just about wearing a cool outfit and running out onto the field. It was about hard work, commitment, and learning to be a part of something much bigger than himself. But Joe was ready. This was the task he had been planning for his whole life.

When Joe first arrived at the Bengals' training facility, he felt like a kid walking into the world's biggest playroom. The field was huge, the grass was perfectly green, and there were footballs everywhere! But it wasn't just about having fun—he knew he had to prove himself. Joe was the new guy, and even though everyone was excited to have him, he needed to show the team that he was ready to lead them to win.

His first day at practice was a mix of joy and nerves. Joe met his new friends, and they welcomed him with open arms. Some were pros who had been in the NFL for years, while others were younger players, like Joe, just starting their professional careers. The cool part was that everyone believed in him. "You're our guy, Joe!" They'd say, clapping him on the back with enormous smiles. That made Joe feel awesome, like he was exactly where he was meant to be.

At practice, Joe was determined to show everyone what he was made of. He zipped passes across the field, his throws perfectly sharp and on target. The ball whizzed through the air, arriving in the hands of his targets, and each time, they gave Joe a thumbs-up or a high-five. It was like magic, seeing how quickly he fit in with the team. His trainers were also pleased, nodding in support as Joe called out plays and made smart decisions. He was already demonstrating that he had what it takes to be a Bengal.

But being part of the Bengals wasn't just about throwing scores. Joe also had to learn how to be a boss. That meant supporting his peers, helping them improve, and working together to make the best plays. Joe wasn't just there to show off his skills; he was there to help his team win. And that's what made him special—he cared about every single person, from the fastest wide receiver to the biggest blocker. They were family now, and Joe was ready to lead them forward.

One of the coolest things about being a Cincinnati Bengal was getting to play at "Paul Brown Stadium", the Bengals' home turf. Joe had seen the stadium on TV before, but now he was standing right there, looking up at the huge seats that would soon be filled with screaming people. It was a thrilling moment, knowing that one day soon he'd be running out onto this very field with the roar of the crowd surrounding him. The idea of thousands of people shouting his name made his heart race in the best way possible.

Joe had another big moment meeting the Bengals' famous coach, Zac Taylor. Coach Taylor had seen something special in Joe from the start, and now they were finally working together. "You've got the talent, Joe," Coach Taylor said, clapping him on the shoulder. "But more than that, you've got the heart. That's what's going to make you a wonderful Bengal." Those words stuck with Joe. He wasn't just there to be good—he was there to be great.

As the training continued, Joe found himself getting closer to his friends. They would joke around during breaks, telling amusing stories or racing to see who could throw the biggest pass. Joe loved those moments because they revealed that football was about building relationships, not just the game. Even though they worked hard, they always found time to have fun.

But it wasn't all fun and games. Joe had to study hard too. He spent hours watching game videos, learning the Bengals' plays, and figuring out how to beat the other teams. Sometimes, it felt like his brain was a machine, getting all this new information. But Joe loved the task. He knew that on the field, smart was as important as strong and fast.

As Joe's first NFL season approached, he could feel the joy bubbling up inside him. He was about to step onto the field for real, in front of thousands of people, as the Cincinnati Bengals' quarterback. It was a dream come true, but it was also the beginning of a new path. Joe knew there would be tough games ahead, but he was ready to face them with everything he had.

CHAPTER 6: JOE BURROW A HERO ON AND OFF THE FIELD

Joe Burrow isn't just a football superstar—he's a hero both on and off the field. Sure, he can throw the football farther than most people can even dream, and yes, he can lead his team to amazing wins, but that's not the only thing that makes Joe a real hero. He's got a big heart, and he cares deeply about the people around him. Whether he's playing under the bright stadium lights or hanging out with his community, Joe Burrow always finds a way to make a difference.

The Power of Caring: When you think of a football hero, you usually imagine someone scoring goals, making big plays, and celebrating with their team. Joe does all of that, but there's more to his story. Off the field, Joe has been known to use his fame to help others. He's not just a football player; he's someone who cares about making the world a better place.

It started when Joe realized others aren't as lucky as him. He saw that some kids didn't have enough food to eat or warm clothes to wear. Instead of just feeling awful about it, Joe chose to take action. He began talking about how important it is to help others, especially those who might be suffering. When Joe stands up, people listen because he's not just a star athlete—he's a person who truly cares.

Feeding the Hungry: One of the biggest ways Joe helps people is by making sure they don't go hungry. After winning the Heisman Trophy, which is one of the most important awards in college football, Joe didn't just talk about football in his acceptance speech. Instead, he spoke about how kids in his city of Athens, Ohio, often didn't have enough food to eat. His speech was compelling that it motivated people all over the country to give money to food banks and organizations that help people in need. In just a few days, thousands of dollars were raised, all because of Joe's loving heart.

Can you picture that? One simple speech about helping others made such a big difference! Joe's words didn't just fill bellies; they also filled hearts with hope. He showed everyone that even a football player can be a hero in the real world.

Leading with Humility: Joe Burrow's leadership style is another thing that makes him a hero. Sure, he's the quarterback, the star of the team, but he's not the kind of guy to shout orders or act like he's better than anyone else. Joe is humble. That means he treats everyone with care, no matter who they are.

When friends are down, Joe is the first to cheer them up. He's always there with a positive word or a high-five, telling everyone that they're all in it together. And this isn't limited to football fields! Joe believes in pulling people up off the field, too. Whether it's through backing local businesses, helping kids chase their dreams, or giving back to his community, Joe shows that being a leader is about helping others succeed.

A Friend to All: If you met Joe in real life, you'd probably be shocked at how friendly and down-to-earth he is. Despite being an NFL star, he's never too busy to stop and chat with fans, sign autographs, or take pictures with young hopeful players. He remembers what it was like to be a kid thinking big, and he wants to show everyone that with hard work and kindness, anything is possible.

Joe loves sharing his story with young kids, especially those who might be going through tough times. He says you can achieve your dreams if you believe in yourself, regardless of your background. Joe is live proof that a small-town kid can grow up to be a sports hero, and he's excited to help the next generation reach for the stars.

Joe's Superpower: Being Kind Being a sports hero is cool, but Joe's real talent is his kindness. Whether he's making a perfect pass or helping someone in need, Joe knows that being kind is the most important thing you can do. He wants to be the best possible person, not the flashiest or loudest.

Through his deeds, Joe shows that real heroes aren't just the ones wearing capes or scoring scores. They're the ones who take the time to help others, show kindness, and inspire people to be better. Joe Burrow might wear a football shirt, but his real hero costume is his big heart.

Inspiring the Next Generation: Joe Burrow's story isn't just about football—it's about using your skills to make a positive effect on the world. He's shown that no matter where you come from or what difficulties you face, you can make a difference. And the best part? You don't need to be a football player to do it!

Joe's trip from a small town to NFL fame is amazing, but his biggest impact will always be the way he's pushed others to care for their communities and work hard for their goals. He's more than just a player—he's a hero that kids everywhere can look up to. With his kindness, guidance, and commitment, Joe Burrow continues to be a bright example of what it truly means to be a hero, both on and off the field.

Joe's Impact on His Team

From the moment Joe Burrow stepped onto the football field, something special started to happen. His friends felt it; the teachers saw it; and even the fans noticed it from the stands. Joe wasn't just any player; he was a boss. But not the kind who shouts and orders people around. No, Joe's leadership was different. He led by example—by working hard, never letting up, and always believing in his team, even when the chances seemed impossible.

Imagine being in the locker room right before a big game. The stress is in the air, and everyone is nervous. But then Joe walks in. His cool, confident smile lights up the room, and suddenly, the jitters start to fade. Joe knows just what to say to his friends. His support, pats on the back, and encouragement say they can do it!

It's like magic—he makes everyone feel better and more confident, just by being himself.

Joe didn't just play for himself; he played for his entire team. He knew that football is more than just one guy running with a ball. It's about teamwork, trust, and helping each other to be the best. When Joe threw a pass, it was as if he was saying to his target, "I believe in you; go catch it!" And when someone scored a touchdown, Joe was the first to cheer. That's how much he loved his team.

Lifting Everyone Up: One of Joe's greatest talents was lifting others. If one of his peers was feeling down because of a mistake, Joe was right there to support them."Don't worry, we'll get it next time!"" he'd say, flashing that big grin. And somehow, that little bit of support would make all the difference.

During training, when things got tough, Joe never let anyone give up. He'd run extra laps with the guys who were struggling, staying late to help others work on their skills. It wasn't just about winning for Joe—it was about making sure his whole team grew. He knew that if every player got better, the team would be unbeatable.

His teachers often said that Joe had a heart of gold. He didn't just care about getting awards or setting records (even though he did both!). He cared about each and every person on his team, from the star players to the guys who didn't always get much time on the field. To Joe, every player mattered, and that's what made his team feel like a family.

The "Never Quit" Attitude: Another thing Joe brought to his team was his "never quit" attitude. In sports, there are times when everything seems to go wrong. Maybe the other team is ahead by a lot of points, or perhaps your own team has made a few mistakes. But Joe never let those times bring him down. He was always the one saying, "We can still do this!" And when Joe said it, you believed it.

There was one game in particular that everyone still talks about. Joe's team was losing at halftime, and the mood in the locker room was pretty gloomy. But Joe wasn't about to give up. He stood up in front of everyone and said, "We've been here before, guys. We know what to do. Let's get out there and play like we know we can." His voice wasn't loud, but it was full of confidence and heart. The team went back out, and sure enough, they turned the game around and won! It was times like these that showed just how much Joe's guidance meant to his team.

Leading by example: Joe wasn't just a leader in the way he talked to his friends; he was a leader in the way he played the game. He worked harder than anyone else on the field, giving 100% in every drill, every play, and every game. His peers couldn't help but follow his example because they saw how much heart and soul Joe put into sports. He was the kind of player who made everyone else want to be better just by watching him.

Even when Joe got knocked down—and he did get knocked down sometimes—he always got back up. And when his friends saw him get up, brush the dirt off his uniform, and keep playing, they felt moved to do the same. No matter how tough things got, Joe never gave up. He showed his team that it's not about how many times you fall but how many times you stand back up.

A Team That Feels Like Family: With Joe on the team, everyone felt like they belonged. He made sure of it. He was the kind of guy who asked the younger players to hang out after practice, knew everyone's birthday, and made people laugh when they were stressed. His friends often said that Joe had a way of making you feel like you were part of something bigger than just a football team. He made you feel like a member of a family.

And that's what made Joe Burrow so special. He wasn't just a talented football player—he was a talented friend. He brought out the best in everyone around him, and because of him, his team wasn't just a group of players trying to win games. They were a group of friends, a family, working together, encouraging each other, and trying to be the best they could be.

Joe's influence on his team wasn't just about the touchdowns he scored or the games he won. It was about the way he made everyone around him feel—confident, capable, and part of something great. And that's what made Joe Burrow a true star, both on and off the field.

Joe Giving Back to His Community

Joe Burrow wasn't just a hero on the football field—he was a hero off the field too. As awesome as he was at throwing scores, Joe cared just as much about helping people in his neighborhood. He knew that being a football star gave him the power to do something beneficial for the world, and he was more than ready to step up!

Let's take a trip to Athens, Ohio, the place Joe calls home. Athens isn't the biggest town in the world, but it's filled with people who have huge hearts, just like Joe. Ever since he was a little kid, Joe felt tied to his city. Even as he became a famous football player, he never forgot about Athens and the people who helped him along the way.

Joe's Famous Heisman Speech: One moment that made everyone in Athens proud was Joe's Heisman Trophy speech. The Heisman Trophy is one of the biggest awards a football player can get, and Joe was super excited to win it. But instead of just talking about how pleased he was, Joe used his speech to talk about something much more important—helping others.

When Joe stood up to give his speech, he didn't talk about his scores or his big wins. Instead, he took a deep breath and talked about the people in his neighborhood who were suffering. He stated how many families in Athens didn't have enough food to eat. He spoke with so much heart that everyone watching could feel how much he cared.

After the speech, something amazing happened. People from all over the country heard Joe's words and were moved to help. Donations started coming in to help food banks in Athens. Because of Joe's kindness, hundreds of families got the food they needed, and it all started with a simple, emotional speech. Isn't that incredible?

Starting the Joe Burrow Hunger Relief Fund: But Joe didn't stop there. He knew that his words could make a difference, but he also wanted to take action. So, he decided to make something special—the Joe Burrow Hunger Relief Fund. This fund was meant to help people in Athens and the nearby areas who were battling to put food on the table.

Joe worked with local organizations and groups to make sure that the money raised went straight to those who needed it most. Every time someone gave, they were helping Joe's goal to fight hunger in his city. Joe's fund made such a huge impact that it encouraged others to start helping out in their own areas too!

What's even cooler is that Joe didn't do this because he wanted attention. He did it because he truly cared about the people in Athens. He knew what it meant to be part of a society and wanted to eradicate hunger in his town.

Helping Kids Just Like You: Joe's love for his neighborhood wasn't just about helping adults—he wanted to make a difference in the lives of kids too. Joe often visited schools to talk to students about the value of working hard, keeping upbeat, and believing in themselves. He knew that being a role model meant showing kids that they could do amazing things, just like he did.

When Joe would visit schools, the kids would light up with joy! Imagine having a football legend come to your school, cheering you on and telling you that you could achieve your dreams.

Joe didn't just talk about sports; he also talked about how important it was to be kind, to help others, and to never give up, even when things got tough.

Joe felt that every kid was empowered to change the world, and he wanted to make sure they knew that. He spent time signing autographs, taking pictures, and answering questions, but most of all, he made sure each kid left feeling inspired and hopeful.

Spreading joy during the holidays: Joe also gave back to his community by sharing joy during the holidays. Every year, Joe would work with local nonprofits to help make sure families in need had a special holiday season. He gave toys, food, and even his time to bring smiles to kids' faces.

One year, Joe dressed up as Santa Claus for a Christmas event! Can you imagine seeing Joe Burrow, the football great, in a big red suit and a Santa hat, giving out presents to kids? It was a sight to see! Joe loved making the holidays special for everyone, and he made sure that no kid was left out.

For Joe, the best part of being a football player wasn't the fame or the trophies—it was the chance to make people smile. Whether he was bringing presents or serving food at a local shelter, Joe always found ways to give back, and that's what made him a true hero.

A Heart Full of Kindness: Joe's kindness wasn't something he did for attention or praise. It was just who he was. He always felt that football was more than just a game—it was a way to connect with people and make the world a better place. Joe used his stage to shed light on important issues and show others that we can all make a difference.

Even though Joe was a big sports star, he never forgot where he came from. He knew that being a hero didn't mean just scoring touchdowns—it meant using his skills and fame to help those who needed it most. Joe's heart was as big as his dreams, and he made sure to fill it with love and kindness for his community.

A Role Model for Us All: Joe Burrow's road to becoming a football star is full of exciting times, but what makes him truly special is his kindness and his commitment to giving back. He didn't just want to be a sports hero—he wanted to be a hero in life. And for the people of Athens, Ohio, and for kids everywhere, that's exactly what he is.

Joe's story shows us that it's not just about what you achieve but how you use your successes to help others. He's a star on and off the field, and his impact will be remembered for the kindness he showed to his community and the difference he made in the lives of so many people.

CONCLUSION

Joe Burrow's story is one that can inspire kids everywhere. It's not just about being talented at football, though Joe is definitely amazing on the field. It's also about the type of guy who is off the game. From a young age, Joe learned that hard work, drive, and kindness could take him far. He also showed the world just how far they could take him!

Growing up in a small place like Athens, Ohio, Joe was just like any other kid. He loved playing sports, hanging out with his friends, and having big dreams. But what made Joe different was that he didn't just dream—he worked hard to make those goals come true. He spent countless hours training, pushing himself to get better, even when things got tough. If he wanted to be the best, Joe had to work hard.

But Joe's journey wasn't just about football. Sure, he became a sports star, but along the way, he also learned important lessons about life. He learned how to be a leader, how to stay upbeat when things didn't go his way, and how to help others. These are things that anyone can learn, whether they want to be a sports player or something entirely different.

When Joe won the Heisman Trophy, one of the biggest awards in college football, he could have talked about his outstanding season, his scores, or all the games he won. But instead, Joe talked about something much more important: the people in his neighborhood. He wanted to help families who were suffering, and his words made a big difference. People all over the country were moved by Joe's kindness, and they stepped up to help, just like Joe did.

Joe didn't stop there. He started the Joe Burrow Hunger Relief Fund to make sure that people in his neighborhood had enough to eat. For Joe, being a football star wasn't just about winning games—it was about using his success to make the world a better place. He knew that his position could help others, and he wanted to give back to those who supported him along the way.

What's even more amazing is how much Joe cares about kids, just like you do. He loves visiting schools and talking to students about working hard, staying upbeat, and being kind to others. Joe knows that every kid is empowered to make a change, and he wants to support you to chase your dreams, just like he did. Whether you want to be a football player, a teacher, an artist, or anything else, Joe's story shows that with hard work and kindness, you can achieve outstanding things.

One of the most enjoyable things Joe does is give back during the holidays. Imagine this: it's Christmas time, and Joe Burrow is dressed up as Santa Claus, giving out presents to kids. That's right—Joe loves to spread holiday cheer, and he makes sure that every kid has something to smile about. Whether he's giving toys, food, or his time, Joe always finds ways to help others and make their days a little better.

But Joe's effect goes beyond just his city. He's become a role model for kids all over the world. His story proves you can win without being the biggest or strongest. What really matters is what's in your heart. Joe's heart is full of kindness, and he uses his success to lift others up, especially those who need it the most.

And it's not just about what Joe has already done—it's about what he's going to do in the future. Joe has big dreams, not just for himself, but for his neighborhood and the world. He wants to keep making a difference, both on and off the field. He wants to show kids like you that anything is possible if you work hard, stay positive, and always remember to help others along the way.

So, what can we learn from Joe Burrow? First, we learn that it's important to follow your dreams, even when the road gets tough. Joe didn't become a sports star overnight. He worked hard, practiced every day, and never gave up, even when things didn't go his way. He showed us that success doesn't come easy, but it's always worth it if you're willing to put in the work.

Second, we learn that being a winner isn't just about winning games or getting awards. It's about being kind, helping others, and making a positive effect on the world. Joe's story is filled with times where he chose to lift others up, whether it was by donating to food banks, visiting schools, or giving back during the holidays. He showed us that real success comes from the heart.

And finally, we learn that no matter where we come from, we all are empowered to make a change. Joe grew up in a small town, but that didn't stop him from thinking big and working hard to achieve his goals. He tells us that it doesn't matter if you're from a big city or a small town—you can make a big impact on the world if you believe in yourself and stay true to your ideals.

Joe Burrow's journey is far from over. He's already achieved so much, but there's no question that he's going to keep inspiring people for years to come. Whether he's throwing scores on the football field or helping families in need, Joe's story is one of kindness, hard work, and determination. And the best part? His story isn't just his own—it's a story that can inspire all of us to be the best versions of ourselves.

So, as you read Joe's story, know that you too can make a difference. Though not a football player, you have unique skills and goals. Just like Joe, you can work hard, stay kind, and use your success to help others. And who knows? Maybe one day, your story will inspire someone else to chase their dreams, just like Joe's tale has inspired you.

GLOSSARY

Athlete: A person who is really good at sports and loves to play! Training hard and improving skills helps athletes excel.

Champion: Someone who wins a competition, like a sports game or a tournament! Champions are often praised and looked up to for their successes.

Determination: This is when you really want to achieve something and don't give up, even when it gets tough. It's like a superhero power that helps you keep going!

Dreams: These are the big goals or dreams you have for the future. It could be anything from wanting to be an astronaut to a sports star!

The Heisman Trophy is given to the nation's top college football player. What counts most is what's in your heart.

Inspiration: This is when someone or something inspires you to do better or try harder. It's like a spark that lights up your goals!

Kindness: Being nice and caring to others. Kindness can be as simple as giving, helping, or saying something kind to someone.

Leadership: The power to help or inspire others. Leaders help teams work together and make choices that benefit everyone.

Perseverance: This means sticking with something, even when it's hard. If you keep trying and don't quit, you're showing persistence!

Role Model: A person who others look up to because of their actions and successes. Role models set a positive standard for others to follow.

Teamwork: Working together with others to achieve a shared goal. It's like being part of a superhero team where everyone has a special role!

Volunteer: Someone who helps others without getting paid. Volunteers often give their time to help their community or support a worthy cause.

Winning: The joy of being the best or achieving a goal. Winning feels great, but it's also important to have fun and play fair!

Community: The people who live in the same place and help each other. Communities are like big homes where everyone cares for one another.

Hard Work: Putting in the work and dedication to achieve your goals. Hard work is what helps you improve and hit new heights!

Made in United States
Troutdale, OR
04/27/2025

30928500R00066